Manage Up!

The Ultimate Guide to Managing Your Manager

Acknowledgments

To my parents, AnnaLee and Albert Ross, for always being my cheerleaders, accepting me for who I am and loving me for it!

To my sister, Greer, for your continuous love and support!

To my former manager, role model, and major inspiration, Lydia Todd!

To my motivational and coaching guru, Tony Robbins!

To my exceptional and talented editor, Lee Hershey!

To my partner in love and life, major encourager, and my endless promoter, defender and champion, Nancy Laviero! Thank you for always being there!

About the Author

Jacqueline Ross is a certified professional career coach, an HR Director,
motivational speaker, and presenter.
Coach Jackie coaches professionals
who are developing their leadership
skills or are in career transition. She
lives in Newton, MA with her life
partner, where she enjoys nature,
hiking, running, and the beach.

Introduction

Well, timing is everything, so they say, and certainly, the timing of writing about managing your manager could not have come at a more interesting juncture. The last eight months or so has been fraught with public exposure of the inherent abuses that have existed, and still exist, for women and men in our workplaces. Abuse of power, harassment in all forms, horrific invasion and intrusion on a person's dignity has been prevalent in our day-to-day news. This book is not in any way intended to address such workplace violence and abuse; rather the purpose of this book is to empower and enrich your tool belt with strategies and tips on how to best navigate your workplace, career, and simultaneously your manager. In the event that you are experiencing workplace abuse and violence. I implore you to seek advice and support in order to address and deal with your unfortunate situation. As a Human Resource Director, I would advise you to please elevate and share your experience with a trusted individual either inside or outside of your organization.

This book originated from sections of the leadership and supervisory trainings that I have conducted over the years on how to manage your manager. In my coaching practice, I have had a large number of clients raise the issue of their daily challenges and struggles on dealing with difficult bosses. So, I decided that I would craft a book geared toward identifying ways to handle your manager. To be transparent, I have had relatively great experiences with most of my managers; however, I know that I have always been fairly strategic about how I have dealt with them. You will learn my secrets of this important skill.

I have had mostly exceptional relationships and experiences with my bosses—with only a couple who were, let's say, less than fun to work within my almost 30 years as an adult in the workforce. And I have had one long-standing manager, for sixteen years, who is someone I admire and owe a great deal of my success. This amazing woman and leader is Lydia Todd, who is currently the Deputy Commissioner of the Department of Probation for the State of Massachusetts. Her work ethic and lived integrity are remarkable. One of her popular phrases and practices is "do as you say, say as you do and you will sleep well at night." Lydia ascribes and lives those values.

But, the reason that I hold Lydia so dear as a manager is that she allowed me to be me. Interestingly, Lydia managed me in a similar way to how my parents parented me. I was fortunate in the sense that I was always encouraged, always allowed and given permission to express myself and be Jackie. I recognize how that climate has shaped me to be the person I am in all realms of my world: individually, professionally and societally.

Now, I don't mean to imply that having a "fabulous manager" in and of itself is going to give you what you need. You have a huge part in how your manager exudes their managerial and leadership magic with you and this book illustrates specific ways in how you can pave the way to assisting your manager in best supporting and managing you. I hope you find these strategies helpful and that you are able to bring the best of yourself and get the most out of your workplace experience.

Best wishes – Your Coach Jackie

Table of Contents

Chapter 1

Know Yourself.
Know What You Need.
Know How to Get It.

There is an adage that says employees leave their manager, not the organization. The manager is seen as the face—and often the voice—of the organization from the perspective of the employee. However, the statement is controversial and new research has shown that good leadership does not reduce employee turnover because of good leadership.

"What we discovered was surprising. Good leadership doesn't reduce employee turnover precisely *because of* good leadership. Supportive managers empower employees to take on challenging assignments with greater responsibilities, which sets employees up to be strong external job candidates. So employees quit for better opportunities elsewhere—better pay, more responsibility, and so on. There is a silver lining, though. Former employees with good bosses are what we call 'happy quitters.'"[1]

The impact of leadership and its relationship to employee retention is debatable. However, employees developing the skill of managing their manager remains critical.

---

1   Gajendran, Ravi and Somaya, Deepak. *"Employees Leave Good Bosses Nearly as Often as Bad Ones." Harvard Business Review. https://hbr.org/2016/03/employees-leave-good-bosses-nearly-as-often-as-bad-ones*

The genesis of this book comes from my years of training "to be" supervisors, supervisors, and managers on how to be most effective in their role as a leader. As part of my leadership trainings, I would create a framework focused on knowing yourself, knowing your job, and knowing your supervisees, yet I was always inclined to note the importance of managing your manager as well. I would not spend an extensive amount of time on managing your manager, but I know the reaction that I would get from attendees when it comes up during my leadership trainings. They would almost have this look of curiosity, and then it would click—an aha moment—an affirmation indicating a definitive realization that, yes, managing their manager is a skill and one to master. I would bring it up in brief discussions and highlight a few of the concepts identified in this book. Interestingly, since I have been a professional leadership and career coach, I have found a number of my clients struggling with just this issue of dealing with their boss and attempting to manage up. I decided it would be worthy to craft a guide so that individuals at all levels of a company or organization could develop and enhance their tool belt in order to manage their boss.

In 1995, I was five years into my career within the mental health field and I was promoted to a program director position overseeing a residential facility for at-risk youth. My previous roles were as a direct care counselor and then an assistant program director working with those same youth. Both of these roles placed me in positions where my *boss*, and my *manager* was always on-site. And even though I had been in one other management position, my manager was always physically present to troubleshoot, brainstorm with, and guide me when I needed his support. Things changed dramatically when I became a program director and no one prepared me for the new experiences I was going to face. In my new role, I was responsible and oversaw twenty employees and was the top manager on site. I had to make independent decisions as to whether I would need to elevate issues for consult, provide my manager, and inform him of critical information or determine when I needed support and guidance. I no longer had someone to talk with right there. I learned quickly that my managers did not have all the answers; in fact, I had to spend time deciphering what their shtick was so that I could figure out who my "go to" people were and how I could access the information I needed to get my needs met and my job done. I realized that

I had to think strategically and figure out how to optimize getting the most out of my boss.

When I began doing leadership and management skills training in 2000, I started to incorporate these concepts as just a *matter of fact* in my discussions. I would address the need to be aware that you cannot be everything to your supervisees, just like your manager cannot be everything to you. I also told them my experience when I had a second rate manager who played favorites. I clearly was not one of them, and he judged me harshly and quickly on my skills without any real observation. I began to develop distrust for him. I had to figure out how I was going to maneuver around this guy. How was I going handle this boss who exercised influence and power over me? I ultimately decided that I was going to return to school and get my master's degree while I continued to work. I had decided that I was not going to be miserable and that I would develop and empower myself through education—which I did.

Over the years, a group of colleagues and I worked together and crafted a curriculum for our supervisory/leadership trainings that would include topics such as, what is the role of a supervisor; how to make the transition into your supervisory role; the challenges you would face as a new supervisor; supervising friends and/or younger employees and supervising older or more experienced employees. We would also launch into various leadership styles and discuss which ones would fit various scenarios more effectively. Professional boundaries, decision-making, and communication skills were also major focus areas and my favorite section was on how to conduct supervisory sessions.

Supervisory sessions are the regular forums between a manager and their supervisee where they would meet to address those particular employees' professional development goals, issues that arose for that employee that they wanted to review, a place to discuss business items such as vacation requests, review policies, etc. A mutual dialogue occurs to provide honest and open performance feedback to support employees' professionalism and effectiveness, allowing for input to be given to the manager as well. This forum may have been more common in the human service industry, as other industries may not have had consistent and regular meetings as described. Most organizations offer feedback to an employee during their annual performance evaluation review process and not in a more immediate and regular format.

These supervisory sessions always allowed managers and employees an opportunity to meet on a regular basis in order to "address issues as they arose" with the intent that the feedback was for improvement purposes and to correct any issues that were interfering in their role. It was during these modules in our leadership training that it dawned on me that we allotted deserved time managing our employees; we also needed to spend time on managing up.

Managing up allows you to gain a sense of control and feel more empowered in your employment situation. I often hear my coaching clients report a feeling of being "stuck," or being unfulfilled in their work situation. Although I could never dictate what people should do and understand that our work allows for our livelihood, one should never take a victim mentality. There are always openings for areas that we have control over and when it comes to our work situations we certainly have areas that we have absolute control. My goal is that you will be able to identify where and how you can regain, reclaim, and possess those reins in your work situation. My strategies may not fit every situation and every personality style and type, however, the more you place yourself in a mindset and "state" of control, the more in control you will feel and will be.

I was working with Lorna, a coaching client, who came to me because her professional goal was to become an HR director and she wanted to work with a coach to help her get there. At the time, she was currently working as a recruiter and when we started meeting she had a boss who curtailed her ability toward any success or movement in her career, so Lorna believed. Lorna almost *surrendered* to her boss's lack of investment in her, which also turned into a lack of investment she had in herself. Lorna knew what she wanted. She could identify some of the steps that she needed to take in order to get there, but she succumbed to her boss's pace. Her boss would entertain Lorna's notions of wanting to step into a role similar to her boss's own and would *allow* Lorna to talk about her desire to become an HR director. But her boss would never give Lorna the opportunity to start to learn and practice the skills to get there. Lorna's boss would verbally encourage her, even affirm her ability to get there, however, in very indirect ways she would thwart Lorna's access and always put her off to a later date and time. My client started making decisions that would lead her to obtain the skills and education she required to propel her trajectory in her HR director direction. She started listening to her inner voice.

Your inner voice, that metaphorical tap on the shoulder you get when your true self is speaking, saying, "Hey, listen up! I have something very important to share and you must listen!" That voice speaks the truth, reminding us of when we are "on or off track." It's the voice that guides us to be honest about who we are and what we were meant to do. We must honor that part of ourselves and allow the messages to be heard. My client had been wrestling with her boss's external control of her destiny rather than staying true to her own known direction. Lorna eventually won out and gave herself permission to be true to herself. She is now sitting in her former boss's position as the HR director and is enjoying every minute of it. Sounds simple? Well, it really wasn't. It took a lot of hard work and commitment, and a firm decision to sit in the driver's seat.

How do you become the pilot of your own professional jet? You must want to know yourself, decide, and commit. I believe that our true purpose is just that: to figure out our true purpose. What is it that we are destined to do? What is our true calling? What are our innate talents and gifts that we are supposed to share with the rest of the world? We are all seeking work to figure this out and some of us tap into it and embrace our true calling more easily or more quickly than others. Many of us continue to work on defining it throughout our lifetime.

I know that I have spent a lot of time trying to wrap my hands around my true purpose and I mostly have it figured out. I know for sure that human behavior and helping others to become their best and true self is a piece of my innate calling. And once you decide what it is that you are meant to do—and sometimes we just have to decide and make that call—our job, then, is to commit to moving in that direction. It is only through commitment that will we ever really know for sure. We have to test it out to see if it truly fits. It is like clothes: we can look at them on a hanger or in a magazine, but it is only when we actually put them on our body do we see if they were meant for us.

As we explore, we begin to determine our direction. It is when we allow ourselves to entertain our outrageous notions; ideas and dreams; and be willing to explore and experiment with them that we determine what sticks, feels right, and fits us. This book is not intended to find your true purpose. Rather, it will provide you with strategies of how to navigate the relationship that you have with the person identified as your *boss* and *manager*. This guidebook will allow you to reclaim your ability to fly your own professional aircraft and obtain greater personal power.

Chapter 2

You cannot be everything to your manager. Just like your manager cannot be everything to you.

Most people, including managers, want to be effective in their job and have a desire to make everyone happy. They often fall into the trap of wanting to be everything to everybody. Unfortunately, that desire is a recipe for disaster. Why? Because it is impossible. We do not have the capacity or ability to be everything to everybody, nor will we always make everyone else happy. Let's start by abolishing this as a goal.

As an employee, know that you, too, are human and cannot be everything to your manager. Nor can you make your boss happy all the time. Although your job and relationship are professionally based and your overarching goal is to be as effective in your role as possible, they are not exclusive of one another. The best course is to focus on obtaining the knowledge, skills, resources, and information you need to be as effective as you can be and in a way that is reflective and naturally you.

What are some of the pitfalls in believing that we can be everything to everybody? First, we may set ourselves up for a goal that is doomed to fail. Now if this sounds too extreme, consider if our efforts are in the hands of someone else, rather than in our own control. Our efforts may lose their potency and impact. I have an example of a former coaching client, Gary, who for years ran a family business that managed office administrators. Gary was a gentle and caring. He struggled with giving his employees feedback when their work performance was poor. He was afraid that they would not like him and that they would get upset with him. After several coaching sessions, Gary came to realize that he was being fearful. Gary's tendency to avoid conflict showed up when he perceived a situation might go haywire; he worried that by giving his employees constructive feedback about their performance might make them feel insulted or not like him. He recognized that by avoiding these discussions and not addressing performance issues with his employees his company was impacted and reflected poorly on him, his business, and his reputation. After some coaching work, Gary found a way to address his employees in a way that was sensitive and direct. Gary found the most natural way to support his employees doing their best.

Another factor about why trying to make everyone happy will inevitably fail is that it drains our energy and burns us out quickly. Today, work roles are varied; we may be responsible for a variety of tasks or have oversight with multiple layers, wherein prioritizing becomes critical. We could end up expending a lot of energy focusing on areas that will have less impact while other more important responsibilities are left by the curbside.

We can also miss out on what is important. Our focus, our target, and direction determine where we are heading and where our attention is paid. If this is misdirected, we can leave out accomplishing critical tasks. Gary, as noted above, spent a lot of time in his own head wanting things to be different in his office. He internalized these conversations instead of having the conversations with his employees. Once Gary decided that he had to use a different strategy and began vocalizing his concerns, he realized that although his employees were not thrilled to get critical feedback, they did adjust to Gary's new style and approach. The end results were that his employees' work and performance improved and his original assumptions were disproved. He was not making everyone happy by avoiding conflict; he was jeopardizing his employees' and business' success.

What may influence or contribute to our desire to please? I know that there are a host of reasons that would contribute to our need to please, which include our personality tendencies, our innate desire to be liked and accepted by others, our need for recognition and praise. Our desire to be a people pleaser also taps into our need to contribute and to give to others in a meaningful way. But it may also reflect our lack of confidence, our fears, and doubts.

There are times when our insistence on focusing on others is a way to eliminate us from the equation. We may not feel worthy or valuable and so we fulfill our identity through giving too much of ourselves to others. We will find, over time, that if our output is constantly focused on others, we will lose our own stamina and sense of purpose.

Now, don't get me wrong, performing well in our roles is super important. It is the "how" you get there, the secret sauce you employ, that is critical. One of my suggested remedies, or part of my secret sauce, has been to **"Jackify"** my roles, a term I coined over the years to describe my approach to my work. "Jackifying", in essence, is bringing my authentic and genuine self to my role. It is bringing Jackie with me all the time. Everything that I do has a "Jackie" flair, a "Jackie" approach, a "Jackie" way that feels true to my values and personhood. It has been a personal branding strategy that I instituted early in my career without really even knowing that I was doing it. Only through exploration and reflection have I understood what I have been doing all along.

"Jackifying" is also about setting the tone and being intentional about my attitude. In addition, to bringing myself into what I do, I ensure that I have an intention about how I want to be when I show up. What type of energy do I want to introduce? What type of tone and attitude do I want to emit? And how do I want others to experience me? These questions have helped me decide that I can ultimately control my day, my focus, and essentially how it will flow.

Another way that "Jackifying" is experienced is that others see you as a unique person they can admire or learn from. Now, I know many of us work hard for others not to see us, but why? Who you are and what you have to share is extraordinary. We would otherwise lose out on being able to see and experience all that you bring to the world. I give the world the opportunity to see me as I really am; all of my goofy and corny parts, too. In my experience, this has been pretty well received.

I was honored to interview Werner Krings, Executive Coach, and Director of Corporate Relations of the Henley Business School in Germany[2], to get his perspective on managing up. Werner relayed that his

---

2 *Werner Krings. https://www.linkedin.com/in/wernerkrings/*

best advice is to adjust to the person who is managing you. Keep to their pace and style. He stated that if you have a mature manager they will allow you and feel comfortable with you working within your own style and will not be intimidated by your individual and unique efforts.

But, just to be clear I don't want folks to get the impression that everyone appreciates who I am. Of course there are some people that don't get me or don't want to get me, and frankly, that is okay. I do not need everyone to like me or connect with me. We are all works of art: everyone's tastes and preferences are different, which means that some will be intrigued and allured by us, some will think we are *meh*, and others would never imagine hanging us on their walls. Totally fine! What we find is that when we are living our true authentic personalities, we bring those to us that connect and gel with us. That is what "Jackifying" is all about.

"Jackifying" becomes important as you move more into yourself. We each evolve into ourselves in very different ways, over periods of time, and through various methods. When we "Jackify", we allow ourselves to come from a place of sincerity and authenticity. In my coaching practice, I work with many professionals who are currently in what I call a "career funk or career misery." They are working to make a living and are removed from doing the things that excite them. And most of the time, when I ask folks what they would really love to do if there were no obstacles or barriers, they never hesitate in their answer. Most people know what they would want to do that would be more fulfilling. It is those things that feel more natural and satisfying.

Another reason that "Jackifying" is important is that people get to experience you, as you, and not as an ideal. Everything that we do is relational; we are connecting with people each and every day, regardless of the nature of our work. We connect in a whole host of ways and in order to achieve a level of success folks need to like you. The organization, BNI, Business Networking International[3], is a global business networking entity with a mission "to help members increase their business through a structured, positive, and professional *referral marketing* program that enables them to develop long-term, meaningful relationships with quality business professionals."

BNI also promotes that in order to obtain those meaningful relationships you need to establish visibility that will lead to credibility and then

---

3   Business Networking International-Massachusetts. bnimass.com

to profitability. Even if you are not a small business owner these concepts apply as well. How you show up in the workplace, the experience people have with you day to day, will determine your level of "likability," which will then determine your credence and level of effectiveness. Bringing you to the table each and every day allows you and others to experience your exquisite and unique self.

So, how do you do that whether or not you are working in your destined field or living and doing the work you are truly passionate about? First, it starts with knowing yourself. Yes, I know that seems simple, but it is true. In order to bring yourself to the workplace, you must know who you are and what you have to offer. One suggested way is to get a better sense of your innate gifts and talents. I suggest a tool I use in my coaching practice called Strengths Finder through Gallup.[4]

I like to use this assessment as it provides some good information and relevant language I can use with clients when discussing their strengths. It is a way to focus on developing the skills so you can gain the mastery in the areas that come most naturally to you. Or you can use any other assessment tool that may work for you. However, here is the thing about assessment tools, they do not wholly define who you are. They will give you some insight, a way to articulate parts of who you are, identify ways that you operate and may offer insight into what makes you tick. Once you complete an assessment tool and review its finding, it is important to identify what about that report resonates and remains with you. Not all parts of an assessment report may fit. Review it carefully and see what speaks your name.

As you learn more about yourself, you can then become clear about what you bring to the world. What do you have to offer, what skills, abilities, and what characteristics are innate and natural that you want to actualize. I realized in the late 1990s that I really enjoyed being in front of people, teaching, and conducting workshops. I enjoyed getting a group of adults together, engaging them in the material in a fun and experiential way. I was able to offer my experiences, have participants be involved, and be a part of the process. I honestly think I have had more pleasure and enjoyment out of engaging others than anything else. It is almost as though I perform to entertain myself, and inevitability others benefit. It is my enthusiasm and energy that I

---

4   *Strengths Finder, Gallup. gallupstrengthcenter.com*

bring to my presentations that creates a climate for fun learning with an interactive process.

Once you decide and give yourself permission that this is who you are, find a way to present it to the world. Bring it forward for everyone to see. You will have then "Jackified" yourself. Probably the single most important lesson that I have learned through my professional career is that when I am being me I am being my best. When I do what I love, even though I don't love every part every time, there is a flavor that is elicited from within that just comes out and flows. When we are comfortable in our own skin we allow ourselves to find out the truest course. Find your secret sauce and then "Jackify" yourself.

Chapter 3

Your manager has innate natural talents and gifts unique to them.
They also have their shortcomings.

In chapter two, we identified that knowing yourself, developing a level of confidence, and solid self-identity though "Jackifying" were the first steps in managing up; the second step is to know your manager and what makes them special and unique. This chapter will focus on how to get at just that: identifying your manager's *shtick*. Your managers have talents, abilities, and skills that have assisted them in obtaining their current position. Your job is to figure out what talents your managers have. What are they good at? What areas seem to come to them naturally? What skills aid them in their success? What do they do that you admire and wish you could integrate into your role and embrace? Identifying your manager's strengths and innate natural talents will offer opportunities for your professional growth and benefit. Yes, my friends, harness and take advantage of what your manager does well. Become keenly aware of what skills and characteristics your manager possesses in order for you to draw upon and apply. I would consider this approach as a strategic path to learning and optimize from your available resources.

So let's start with focusing on learning and paying attention to your manager. Use your observation skills to identify what makes them stand out? What are the abilities and qualities that assist them in doing their job well? When I was in my mid-20's I was running a residential treatment program for youth and there was a change in the client population. What once worked really well in managing and handling situations was not working at that time. You know when you continue to do the same things and continue to get the same lousy results? Time for a new strategy! And that is just what I did.

But I was stuck; I was not quite sure what my options were as I had landed in this new territory. I knew I needed to ask for help. Asking for help is not a weakness but reveals a strong character. However, be sure to identify the problem and clarify the work issues with which you are struggling.

So, I evaluated and assessed my resources before I reached out. Who was my go-to in this situation? Well, I liked and respected my manager, but when I thought about what she would have to offer, I knew that she would not be the person to help me best. She was gifted in her own way. She knew how to navigate the politics of our funding sources, speak well with stakeholders, and she had excellent writing skills, but my instinct was such that she would not be my best support with the issues that I was struggling with; I began to think of who would be? And as I scanned the resources in my organization, I thought of one person who had really exceptional milieu management skills and called upon him. I told my supervisor that I was going to reach out to this other manager and the reasons why. She had no issue with that and he was able to offer suggestions and methodologies that were helpful. In this situation knowing my manager's strengths and weaknesses really came in handy. It was also important to be aware of the other resources that were out there for me when my manager could not deliver as needed.

It is also been my experience that people like to talk about themselves. There could be multiple reasons why that is the case so, in order to best learn and understand your manager's skill sets and strengths, it may be beneficial to ask your manager what they think they are good at. You may get some good information by giving your manager an opportunity to speak about their skill sets. How did they fall into their career trajectory? What are they hoping to do and become in the future? What are the areas of their job that gets them jazzed up? Of all the great things they do, what are the two to three things that they do exceptionally well? Over the last year, what accomplishments are they most proud of? It is okay to let your manager know that you're interested in learning from them and you should tap into their abilities so you can excel in your role.

You should also consider what is not your manager's *shtick*. Strong and self-confident managers will be open to talking about areas that are not their "thing." So, for example, I would classify myself as a visionary, yet I often miss small details. Getting bogged down in details is something that is really annoying to me; however, as part of my role, I need to be on top of those things as well. One strategy that many managers employ is to hire people around them to complement their strengths and who are skilled in areas that they are not. Ask your manager, what are the areas that are not as exciting or fun for them to do? Are there skills and qualities that don't come naturally? Use your observation skills and pay attention to the things that are not within your manager's skill set. We are all human. We all have our innate talents and gifts that make us unique and we all have areas that we do not excel in. That makes us human and real.

Knowing your manager's skills and talents, both what they are great at, and not so great at, will aid you in a few ways. One important way is it will assist you with your own professional growth. What do I mean by that? Well, in order to best map out your future in advance and take charge of your career, it is important to identify your own professional development needs and interests. There are some folks out there who from the beginning of time know exactly what they were destined to do and there are more of us who are figuring that out along the way. Today there are so many paths to take and many of us are continually changing our career direction and focus. It is truly a journey. There is no one right way. You will be the sole determinant if what you are doing and pursuing feels right. However, investing some time, energy, and focus into exploring what you would like to do will have enormous benefits.

The assessment tool mentioned in the earlier chapter, Strength Finder through Gallup, is a great way to identify areas that you already excel in so you can further work on skills to obtain mastery in those areas. I am a huge fan of focusing your energies on developing skills sets that will enable you to optimize your already given talents while finding ways to manage the areas that are not your thing. However, just knowing your strengths is not enough. You need to continually work on them in order to develop and enhance those areas. It's like working out. You don't just decide one day that you are going to be in shape, work out for one day and then think you are fit. Muscles need continuous work out in order to stay strong and healthy. The same goes for skill growth. But how do we know what to work on? What areas are going to be most important? That is a complex and great question. I would start with the area that gets you most excited and jazzed up.

I was working with a client named Barbara who was in marketing and public relations for a nonprofit organization. She reported being exceptional in her job; she loved to write, was on top of heading the company's social media marketing campaigns, and was an excellent networker. The area that she was struggling with was her relationships with her colleagues and team because she almost had a "my way or the highway" approach with people and folks were turned off. When she came to me for coaching she reported feeling on the verge of getting fired due to her strained work relationships and her reported curt approach towards others. When speaking to her about her other interests and hobbies she shared that she was a yoga instructor, which she simply loved. She talked about how teaching yoga was so fulfilling to her and as we explored the elements of patience, calmness, and engaging her participants in her yoga class, Barbara realized that these were skills she already had and could integrate them into her style with her colleagues in her other work world. Barbara decided that one of her professional development focus areas was to take her yoga instructor teaching and mentoring approaches off the mat and integrate them into her other work world with her colleagues. She reported having great success. Oftentimes, we may realize that we already have these skill sets and abilities that are working in other parts of our lives. Barbara was able to pull and draw from her yoga world in a way that befitted her marketing world.

Another area that will reap benefits is to decipher how your current role will support your career path and route. As you figure out what you can learn from your manager, identify how your current role will support your professional growth. Now you might say my current role has nothing to do with my ultimate goals and ambitions. Okay, that is going to take a personal assessment and evaluation; however, there are always opportunities to learn whether or not you are in your most desired position or situation.

Decide to be a sponge for learning. Regardless of your relationship with your manager, find ways to learn from them. Your manager can provide multiple tools and resources to you as long as you allow yourself to view and perceive them as valuable material to enhancing your professional growth.

Chapter 4

The impression you have of your manager can be your greatest professional opportunity or your greatest professional barrier.

Our beliefs and impressions about our managers drive our actions and attitudes towards them. Sometimes we have these notions about our managers and convictions about who they are and why they are the way they are, but it may have little merit or credence. It is time to challenge and explore those beliefs and impressions, as they can either be serving you well or detracting from your level of effectiveness and contentment in your role. This chapter will allow you the opportunity to explore the beliefs and impressions you hold and if necessary take steps to write a new script about what you believe to be true about your manager.

Tony Robbins stated that "The minute you decide to focus on something, you assign it a meaning and infuse it with a feeling." He continues to say, "That how you define an event produces emotion and determines your inner feeling state going forward. The meaning you assign to any event, interaction or outcome defines the emotional tone of your experience and the feelings you generate throughout your life. Meaning equals emotion and emotion equals life." [5]

---

5 *Robins, Tony. "Why Meaning is Everything." https://www.tonyrobbins.com/why-meaning-is-everything/*

That is a powerful concept and statement. In essence, Tony Robbins is stating that we create the story behind the events in our lives. And our stories breathe life. We designate an impression that is connected to our emotional experience about that event or situation. Our impressions will be imprinted in our memory and the lens in which we view the people involved in that experience. And those meanings become our beliefs and impressions. They become anchored and are experienced within us.

When we attach a meaning to a situation, event, or interaction, we tell our brains what to focus on and what is important. We use a part of the brain called the Reticular Activating System (RAS) where "we notice what matches our internal beliefs and identified contexts." In an article entitled, *The Power of Focus*, Dean Bokhari continues to state that "focus instantly generates ideas and thoughts we wouldn't have had otherwise. Even our physiology will respond to an image in our head as if it were a reality."

Is that correct? Our body will create an experience about something that we just tell it to? Pretty powerful. As David Allen notes in *Getting Things Done*: "Just like a computer, your brain has a search function— but it's even more phenomenal than a computer's. It seems to be programmed by what we focus on and, more primarily, what we identify with. It's the seat of what many people have referred to as the paradigms we maintain." And our brain will find evidence to support what we are focusing on. It does not discriminate and determine whether it is good or bad for us. It will find evidence to support what we tell it.

Bringing this back to our manager, the meaning we give to our interactions with them creates our beliefs and impressions. This, in turn, creates the message that we tell our RAS to focus on and then our switch is turned on to find evidence to support those beliefs. The meaning we create and what we tell ourselves becomes truly important to how we experience our relationship with our manager.

A former client of mine, Gail, has been working for a prominent law firm in Boston as an executive assistant. When she came to me for coaching, her primary goal was to develop a plan to transition into her true calling, which is cooking, however, the present tension and strained relationship with her manager was gnawing at her every day. She said to me that she believed her manager's main purpose in life was to make her life miserable. Gail stated this with conviction. She had been working for this manager for many years and truly believed that he did not like her; he did things purposely to make her life unbearable, and she could cite incident after incident that supported these beliefs and impressions. However, she was eager for this to change and knew she needed to find a way to change this dynamic although she did not know how.

We went through an exercise of identifying her beliefs about her manager, which as you can guess were largely negative. Next, she identified all the experiences, (well not all, but a lot) that supported and showed evidence that her beliefs were true. Gail was still convinced that her impressions were dead on. We then walked through recreating her beliefs about her boss. One of the examples she shared was that he never acknowledged her or said hello when he would walk by her desk. She also said that he would never ask her about how she was doing, how her weekend was, and even how her daughter was doing. She felt that he didn't care about her, was rude and she felt invisible in his presence. As a result, Gail would never acknowledge her boss either. So the two of them would be passing ships in the night; they were both there, but never connecting in a casual and social way, except for business and work matters.

Gail decided that maybe he did care, but expressed it differently. Maybe he wasn't rude and just maybe he wasn't ignorant. Could he possibly be distracted with other things on his mind? Is it possible that he is not a small talker or socializer? When she started asking if there could be other meanings that did not equate to a lack of care or concern for her, she opened up her options of ways she could engage differently. Amidst this conversation, Gail started to strategize what was in her control and what she could do. How could she engage and approach her manager? And she decided that she could say hello; she could ask her manager how his weekend was and how his kids were doing. That she could initiate this dialogue and regardless of his reaction, she would at least know that she was not what she disliked in him. That she was not acting in a way that he could judge or believe negative impressions about her.

Gail tested this out and had some really positive results. She initially shared that the first day she greeted her manager with a warm welcome and an inquisitive conversation with him. He looked like he was in almost shock. She reported that she kept her cool and acted as if this was normal protocol and each time she saw him she acknowledged his presence. In turn, the results were positive. Gail's manager reciprocated and began asking her questions about her, her family, and her weekend. In addition, he offered her Red Sox tickets to a game with his season seats. An offer never before given. So, even though this illustrated a small gesture, a shift in thinking, and change in approach, it actually transformed Gail's experience with her manager in a positive and effective way.

So, what did Gail do? Gail acknowledged, first and foremost, that a change in her relationship with her manager started with her. She identified what impression she had about her manager and if those were positive or negative beliefs. Secondly, Gail reviewed those impressions and asked herself were those underlying beliefs serving her? Did the meanings she held benefit her or detract her from being effective? Did the feelings from those impressions generate satisfaction and serve her well? She then took those negative beliefs and decided to attach a different meaning to them. She opened herself up to think that maybe there was a different explanation to his actions or attitude towards her. And ultimately anchored a different impression in her lens about her manager.

How can you change your impressions and beliefs about your manager and rewrite the script? First, you must believe that you can change the script and that it is only you that can do it. Second, like Gail, you can take a moment and think about what you believe to be true about your manager. How do you view them? What impressions do you have about them? Do these beliefs and impressions serve you well or do they detract from your effectiveness in your role and your professional skin? Write down your beliefs and impressions about your manager. Split the page in half and decide whether those beliefs or impressions serve you well or detract from your effectiveness. Look at the list that is detracting and explore reasons why those beliefs may not have merit or evidence to be true.

The next step is to identify what meaning will serve you better. Now, this exercise does not require one to be living in a fantasy world that does not acknowledge real issues, real problems, and minimizes that there may be weeds among the flowers in the garden. There are weeds and we have to deal with them, but it is truly in the way we decide to script the story with the content, the emotion attached, the intensity level, and the intentions that guide how we deal and manage them. Gail made a choice to guide her relationship with her manager in a new and different way and she allowed a shift in her beliefs and actions toward her manager.

The next step is to identify your expectations and desired outcomes. What is your ideal objective regarding your relationship with your manager? What would you like the connection to look like? Be clear and know that you only have control over your decisions, your actions, and your attitude and engagement with your manager. Develop a plan and execute a new approach based on your new belief and meaning you are going to attach. Put that plan into action so you can anchor your experience and assess to see if and how it is working. Review your progress and determine if you need to course correct. And remember, regardless of the outcome, your ability to stretch and challenge your impressions and identify new meanings that will serve you better.

Chapter 5

What is important to you may be different for your manager and knowing what is important to your manager is critical.

Have you ever considered seeing things from your manager's point of view? Have you ever wondered what are the issues and challenges that they are facing? Are you curious about how are they going to manage and handle them? What keeps your manager up at night? What are they most focused on and worried about? This chapter is going to illustrate the value of knowing the answers to those questions and identifying an approach about how you can use that information.

In chapter three, we discussed that your manager has innate talents and gifts that are unique to them and that knowing their *shtick* is an important element for you to effectively manage up. Additionally, your manager also has worries and concerns, priorities and directives, and knowing those areas can be just as crucial to your relationship with your manager, your insight to the organization's direction, and enhancement to your professional growth. Now, clearly, there may be limitations to what you may learn; however, be open to taking in all the information so that it allows you to crystallize a working framework of your manager's priorities.

Okay, and so what? What if you know your manager's priorities and concerns? Well, there are a few benefits. First, it may enhance your relationship with your manager. Engaging in a genuinely interesting conversation with your manager about their focus creates a co-relationship where there is a give and take. Secondly, it also may give you some insight into what your manager does in order for you to determine if you have sights on a promotion to a similar position. And lastly, it allows you to obtain an aerial perspective of the organization and its direction.

As an employee you have directives, you have a defined role with specific responsibilities. How do we decide what our focus is? When we sit in our seats, assume our positions, we often work in our own bubble and our lens determines our focus. The question is what are the elements that determine that lens and focus? The reality is that the priorities you hold versus your manager may be varied. Your manager has one lens that is often broader, with a bigger picture in mind. They know variables about the business and organization that may be unknown to you. Therefore, their focus is on a different plane. Part of your job is to understand and learn what is important to your manager. So, yes we do have the dual responsibility of knowing our own priorities and learning our managers. But, how do we do that?

Lydia Todd, Deputy Commissioner of the Department of Probation for the State of Massachusetts, and my former manager of 16 years says that one of the first crucial questions you should ask yourself is what is the 10% of your job that my boss is focused on? Deputy Commissioner Todd feels that figuring out our manager's priorities and mastering that "thing" allows us to gain and develop our manager's trust and confidence. She shared that early investment in getting your boss' confidence and asking the right questions, such as what needs to be reported to them versus what doesn't, what are their top three priorities for you this month? What am I not doing that you wish I would do and what am I doing that you wish I would stop? Understanding your manager's priorities and getting the rhythm of trust frees up your time and attention to drive the work that needs to be done.

Most organizations today have identified strategic goals and priorities. Long range and visionary thinking are important where an organization will articulate and craft clear, specific, and measurable goals. It helps set the course and direction for the organization and provides the employees and stakeholders with an understanding of where this company wants to go. This, in turn, makes it even more helpful to employees to know how their role fits into the organization's scheme. A solid, strategically aligned organization will have everyone at all levels support the attainment of those goals, objectives, and its desired destination. So, does your organization have a strategic plan? Have you seen it? Does your manager talk with you about the organization's strategic plans and do they provide insight into your department's role within the plan?

If so, fantastic! You will have a greater awareness and insight into what your organization has identified as its targets. This information will allow you to know if the organization's goals fit into your professional ambitions. If you have not heard or seen the organizations strategic plan, ask your manager if there is one and if so, where could you locate a copy. Some organizations post their strategic plan or send them to employees in an annual report which addresses progress or lack of progress toward attainment of identified goals. Having a sense of alignment with the organization's strategic vision helps you to know if this is the right organizational fit. Can I embrace where my organization is going? Does their direction fit into supporting my growth and development? How can I be a major contributor to the success of the organizational goals?

One strategy a manager of mine had shared with me many years ago was the *80/20 rule*. As I did some exploration into the *80/20 rule* I learned in an article, *Understanding Pareto's Principle—the 80/20 Rule*[6] by F. John Reh[7] at the Italian Economist, Vilfredo Pareto looked at wealth distribution in the United States and he determined that 80% of the wealth was held by 20% of the population. Later in the 1940's, Dr. Joseph Juran used this 80/20 formula and connected it to a management tool and how we could prioritize our work. He used the *80/20 rule* as a framework, as a way to determine work priorities.

Author F. John Reh states, "The *80/20 rule* suggests that we focus on the few larger items that will generate the most significant results." This strategy applied to managing your manager allows you to spend 20% of your time doing the critical priorities from the lens of our managers, as they will produce the greatest outcome. This will then allow us to spend 80% of our time focusing on what we feel is important in order to do our job well. This manager reported that this approach had worked for her

6   Reh, F. John. "Pareto's Principle: The 80-20 Rule." The Balance. https://www.thebalance.com/pareto-s-principle-the-80-20-rule-2275148. 08 Aug 2017.

7   Reh, F. John. https://www.linkedin.com/in/fjohnreh/ t

over the years and felt strongly that the 20% of our time spent on our manager's priorities was time well spent.

Abbey, a project manager in the healthcare industry came to me for coaching to figure out her next career direction. While Abbey and I were working on her career trajectory, she was working for an organization and assisting a physician to build a new practice. Abbey wanted to maintain a strong focus on helping to successfully launch this new practice. She had just been transferred from another practice where there was friction between her and the leading physician and this time she decided she wanted to try a different strategy. So, she delved into learning this new physician's philosophy, values, and direction of his intended goals for the practice. In order to find out what was important to him, she prepared and went to him with some interview questions so she could learn what he had in mind. What was his vision for the practice? What did he want it to look and feel like? Abbey wanted to be able to understand, help to support, and align her focus to his direction. He gave her articles around leadership that spoke to him and practices around patient/client care. Abbey read those articles thoroughly and got a real sense of what was important to this physician, his beliefs regarding patient care and his style as a leader and manager. Abbey was actually pleasantly surprised at how willing the physician was to share his ideas and ones that she embraced pretty easily.

Abbey was armed with information and it made it easier to adjust her priorities to ensure that they aligned and encompassed her manager's focus. Abbey employed that *80/20 rule* as she built a new relationship with her new manager and supported the development of the new practice. Abbey would ensure that the first part of her day entailed working on the areas that were critical and important to her manager, and while doing so, experienced a new collegial form of relationship with her manager that she had not experienced with her previous one.

Abbey illustrates one example of how the *80/20 rule* can be applied. The *80/20 rule* also implies that in order to execute this effectively you must know the significant areas to draw your attention. Organizational strategic plans can give some initial guidance into the company's priorities and speaking with your manager to find out what is important to him or her could bode well. Ask your manager what are their top three areas that keep them up at night and what you could do to assist in addressing and tackling those issues. The more insight you have into their priorities, the better you will be able to strategize and utilize your time.

Chapter 6

Be your own manager by navigating your career direction.

Seizing the reins to guide your career direction takes intention, planning, and execution. It frankly takes some work. But work that can reap some real long-lasting benefits mentally, emotionally, physically, and spiritually. There are some who turn their passions into careers. There are some who inject and incorporate their passions into their everyday lives through hobbies and extracurricular activities, and there are some who are able to blend the two. There is no right or wrong answer or any strict approach. However, one step toward moving in your desired career direction is to know exactly the types of things and activities that jazz you up. What are the things that you do that make you say, "Yes, this is what life is about!" Something that you can continue doing endlessly, something that just makes you feel AWESOME! Now, I know what you are thinking right now. Maybe its surfing Pinterest; or it's art tripping in museums; or its designing spaces, such as offices or homes; or, maybe it's teaching and sharing information and tools with others that you have acquired that excite you. Whatever those things are—and there may be a lot—finding ways to integrate them into our career trajectory will produce multiple benefits.

So, step number one is to identify those activities that jazz you up. Right now, if you are so inclined, grab your journal or computer, find a quiet space, and think about a time that you felt on top of the world.

Recall a time when you felt like whatever you were doing, you were meant to be doing. A time where everything fit into place. This experience triggered feelings that tapped you on the shoulder and said, "This is what life is about. This is exactly where I should be, what I should be doing and it feels amazing!" As you reflect on this time, write down where this occurred. What were you doing? Who were you with? What feelings were emitted? What other details or elements existed in this situation that you recall? Write all of these things down.

Repeat this exercise and identify two more times that you felt like you could not lose, that you were soaring and totally in your element. As you reflect and review these three experiences, identify if there are any themes that emerge. Are there similar activities, elements or qualities in these experiences? Are there any clear commonalities and aspects that stand out? Take a few minutes to jot those down. Review your list. What have you learned? Does anything seem apparent? Are there any takeaways that you have from this exercise? I hope so!

If this has had you a bit stumped or if you want to continue exploring this area, I would recommend that over a two-week period you do an exercise to "catch" your aha and jazzed up moments. By this I mean, jot down things that you find yourself getting really excited about. As you are walking through your day, identify and write down moments that you start to get those internal good feelings. Identify what you were doing, where you were, who you were with, and any other special aspects of the experience. This allows us to be more mindful of each given experience and you can recall small moments that brought you joy. The more we are able to identify what characteristics are a part of the experience, the easier it will be to find ways to duplicate and replicate those situations.

Another strategy that you can use to identify your career direction and goals is to use career guide tools and resources. I always recommend the book, What Color is My Parachute by Richard N. Bolles. This book has been out for over three decades and has a guided workbook that you can take advantage of. I often use this with clients who are stuck and uncertain about their next career steps. The feedback I have received from clients has been positive. The workbook allows you to explore a variety of areas related to career choice and direction.

The workbook moves you through seven exercises that start with your "know how's;" the kinds of people you prefer to work with; your talents, gifts and abilities; your preferred working conditions; the amount of money and level of responsibility you desire; where you want to live; and ultimately your *why*, your reason for being, your mission and purpose. At the end, you gather the key takeaways from each exercise and put them onto one large floral petal, a metaphor of you and all that you encompass, and plot the results so you have a visual representation of your world of work and career preferences and desires. It is a great launch pad that allows you clarity about career focus, direction, and industries to target.

In chapter two, I suggested using the *Strengths Finder* by Gallup as a way to learn your innate talents and gifts. When you buy the book, it provides you with an access code, which will allow you to complete the tool. It will generate a report that will describe your top five themes and will provide you with action steps for each theme to strengthen and develop skills to enhance those themes. A very useful resource. So, if you have completed the Strengths Finder—fantastic. Bridging your talents and interests are a great way to identify career paths and options that would marry things that both excite you and what you are good at. The activities that we enjoy, as well as excel at, most often elicit an awesome feeling.

Now, review your list of activities that jazz you up. How do they compare with your Strength Finder talents and gifts? Are there any natural connections? Identify three of your activities identified that compliment and support your Strength Finder themes. Now test this out. Over the next month, make a commitment to find ways that incorporate these activities. Try them out to see how they "fit and feel." Record in your journal any observation and impressions. If you have completed the exercises above, you probably have a great working list of activities and talents that are suited to you and you have tested some of these out. You also tracked the merging of these two together and have some data about the outcome.

Another strategy to explore your career path is to be intentional. Give yourself permission to reflect and focus on what it is that you want. What will sustain you and make you happy? A common theme that I encounter with many clients is that most (but not all) of them have an inkling and know what it is that they really want. However, usually, they are just full of fear, doubt, insecurities—you name it. And those fears, doubts, and insecurities over time develop and create a life of their own. I do encounter clients that truly don't know what they want or have not allowed themselves the opportunity to really delve in and figure it out. I say, why not? This is your opportunity—your life—to determine and plan your path. The greatest gift about targeting a goal and being intentional is that you get to plan your future in advance. Seize the opportunity and run with it. Look, the reality is that you are going somewhere whether you like it or not. Wouldn't it be better to pick where you want to go, rather than opt out of that decision? I say, pick your course!

Today, technology allows us to find research and locate information within a moment's time and at a fingertip touch. Do your research. Talk to your friends, colleagues, and family members. Interview people that have careers close to areas that you gravitate toward. Invest the time to play and explore this part of your world. You need to, since it is a part of your world that will consume a lot of your time and energy. You may not discover *it* entirely. Many of us today do not have one identified career focus or path; however, you can find "them." There are multiple things that you can do to earn your living and still bring you satisfaction, as well as serve to the betterment of others.

Test your findings out. You never know unless you try. Your ideas will start this journey; however, putting those ideas into action will be the only litmus test to see how they land, fit, and feel. In this chapter we discussed strategies to explore and discover where you want to go and identifying your career focus and direction. In the next chapter, we will discuss other options and resources for further exploration and a continuation of your journey. You may be asking, what does this have to do with managing up? The simple answer may be that the more you know about yourself and the more resourceful that you are, the better able you are to contribute towards your manger's priorities and add to the success of your manager and your organization.

Chapter 7

Mentoring. What is the hubbub?

Resourcefulness is a key ingredient in managing your boss. It is also a key ingredient in helping your career growth and moving you to your desired path. But how do you know where your resources exist and how do you access and use them? These are the questions that we will tackle in this chapter.

In chapter two, we discussed how your manager has innate talents, and, of course, areas that he or she is not particularly skilled in. It is your responsibility to decipher your manager's talents and challenges. Knowing that information is one step, but how you use that information can greatly assist you. One way that it can be helpful is to determine if your manager is truly your professional development ally; meaning, do they really demonstrate and take action to support your professional growth? Are they invested in you gaining the skills, knowledge, and becoming a master of your position? Are they setting you up to eventually learn their job or components of their job? Assessing your manager's genuine interest in your success is the first step in determining how your manager can be a true resource to you.

If you determine that your boss is on your "growth side," then take advantage of their advice and expertise. Ask them for feedback. Share with them your professional ambitions and the skills that you are looking to master. Take the risk of exposing your goals, and by doing so, you let your manager know that you are eager, determined, and interested in growing as a professional. Solicit their feedback and put it to use.

In the event that you determine your manager is not genuinely interested in your professional growth—whether they are overwhelmed in their position, do not possess the skills that you would want to echo, just don't embrace a coaching or mentoring role, or are poor managers—then seek feedback elsewhere. Find a mentor who seems interested in sharing the *knowledge of wealth* inside or outside of your organization. Find someone that you admire and would want to emulate.

Dorie Clark[8], marketing strategy consultant, professional speaker, author, who graciously agreed to be interviewed for this book provided her perspective on managing up. She said that the key ingredient to managing up is a two-pronged approach. She stated first that it is about adopting a mentality that it is your job to make your bosses life easier. If you follow that train of thought, and if you have a good boss, you will then earn their gratitude and it will make them want to help you. She also stated that you would need to simultaneously develop relationships, as well as create and stretch your tentacles into other parts of the organization in order for others to get to know you and understand that you are contributing to your boss's success. Even if you have a challenging boss, this will allow you to turn inside the organization to find help and provide you with internal opportunities.

Mentors are like your guardian angels. They take you under their wing to support and guide you. They innately want to share with you their secrets of success, the choices they made along their path. They want to divulge their learnings and pitfalls, obstacles and barriers they encountered and overcame so that you can be watchful and pivot as necessary. They essentially assist you in laying out your path and offering options of routes you can take. They may serve as your role models; they have "been there" and are willing to share their experience to you. Absorb and incorporate their learnings into your professional life.

Finding a mentor may require you to take the initiative to seek one out. It will take time and effort. Here are three action steps to finding a mentor. First, identify individuals that you know, like, and admire. Second, actively demonstrate your interest in furthering your learning and career. Lastly, ask them.

---

8 *Doris Clark. https://www.linkedin.com/in/doriec/, a*

Step number one is to identify someone—or several individuals—who are doing the job you wish to be doing, possess the qualities that you aspire to and are individuals that you wish to mirror. They may be ten steps above you in their professional career. This may be someone that works either inside or outside of your organization. Whichever the scenario, you can start to identify the person(s) that could be your role models or individuals that possess the skills you are wishing to develop. For example, you may want to seek out individuals who are exceptional leaders, have a strong presence, and articulate a clear and compelling vision. You may want to find someone who exhibits stellar communication skills and uses words that are powerful and thoughtful. You may want to work with someone who makes fact-based and inclusive decisions, and takes consistent and effective action. You may also want to find a mentor who has a strong team that is aligned and committed. And you may want to find someone who is constantly invested in their own knowledge base and actively works on their own professional development and learning. Now, remember, they may not possess every skill area that you are seeking to learn and master, but they may possess some specific areas that will assist you to grow into your next steps. Here are some questions you may want to consider:

• What are the skills that I am looking to master?

• Who excels in those skills?

• What position(s) am I looking to obtain in five years?

• Who currently holds that positions(s)?

• Who possesses a special quality? What makes them unique and stand out in a way that I admire?

These are just some questions that can start your mentoring search criteria. Of course, you can drill down and target a deeper specificity in your questions; i.e. identify more specific skills, jobs previously held, companies they may have worked for, etc. The clearer you are about what you are looking for in a mentor, the easier it may be to identify the person(s) who could help you the most. At the end of this step, the goal is for you to identify potential mentors.

Once you have your identified potential mentors, the second step is to continue your pursuit of professional growth and development. If you are seen and viewed as someone who is actively pursuing your professional development growth, it will show your commitment and dedication to the progress of the company as well. Target your focus on your potential mentors and show this by being of value to them. Assist them in whatever way possible. Respond to their tweets; comment, with substance, on an article they posted on LinkedIn; and offer to assist on any projects they are working on. Find a way to be of service to them. There is a philosophy and adage that says, givers gain. What you put out to the world, you receive back ten-fold. So, be of service, be of value, and look to give first before receiving.

And lastly, go for "the ask." Once you have paved a relationship with this person, and have shown your commitment to your career and to the development of theirs, then ask if they would be willing to take you on in a mentoring role. Do your research and share with them your reason for wanting to work with them. Let them know that you admire a certain skill, their leadership style, and presence or the impact a project had and how you would find it invaluable to absorb and learn from them. If they readily agree to take you on as a mentee then SCORE!

Fantastic. You are on your way to starting a professional journey that can result in endless possibilities. Now, on the other hand, don't get discouraged if they are uncertain or flatly say, no thank you. Taking on a mentee is work for that person. So, chalk it up as a practice round and start to pursue another potential mentor. If you get stuck, go back to step number one and then step number two. Continue this process until you find a mentor match.

Once you have come to an agreement to start this mentoring relationship, remember to keep an open mind, as you will find your mentor will have their strengths and genuine gifts, as well as areas that are not in their wheelhouse. Because one person cannot be everything to us: we are all human. Identify with your mentor an understanding and a mutual agreement about how this mentor/mentee relationship will work. Define the parameters, how often will you meet, what will be the frequency, will you meet in person or remotely, identify what skills and areas that you are interested in tapping into that they do really well. Be specific about your goals. Be open, receptive, and put into action their feedback. Test out their feedback and see how it fits. Remember givers gain, so your mentor will reap benefits from this experience with you as well.

A friend and colleague of mine, Tom Matthews, a successful residential realtor in Concord, Massachusetts, shared with me that being a part of a referral networking organization, BNI (Business Network International), has allowed him to seek out mentors he would not have had the opportunity to in his day-to-day encounters. He reports that it is "important to mention that you need to be in a supportive environment to find mentors." One such mentor that Tom has found is a landscaping owner, Todd Stout, whom Tom met about nine years ago and, as he reports, they hit it off right from the start. Tom went on to say that "Todd really helped me with organizational structure and business ideas." Tom also said that the true essence of the mentor and mentee relationship is when it becomes collaborative, "when the mentee can begin and return ideas to the mentor." The pivotal point is when the exchange and the value of that exchange is a mutually shared experience between both parties.

Mentoring can be found in both formal and informal ways. Whichever route you have pursued, remember mentors are not found in a single individual, but rather in a variety of people who possess different skill sets, strengths, and learning opportunities for you. They can assist in shedding light on your blind spots, they can show you new paths and opportunities, and they can help in building and leading you to create new connections. I would imagine, at some point, after you have had the experience of being mentored, the desire to mentor others will become strong. It will be at that point that you will experience the true value of mentoring.

Chapter 8

Networking for people who dislike networking.

Networking. Yes, I have said that dreadful word, *networking*. Now, I know most of you probably have a disdain for the idea or notion of networking. In this chapter, my goal will be to break down the purpose and strategies to effectively network. Networking can become one of your true allies and part of your career development strategy to assist you in managing your manager.

You may ask: what does networking have to do with managing my manager? Well, it comes down to understanding the essence and definition of networking. Mentoring, as we discussed in chapter seven, is a form of social networking and building relationships. Relationships are the essence of creating opportunities. Networking, in its simplest form, is really about creating and sustaining relationships. That's it. It is relational and frankly, if we think about it more broadly, isn't everything we do about relationships? However, this type of relationship building involves establishing relationships with people who you can use to help advance your career and/or your business. Therefore, developing and creating relationships to obtain resources, skills, and knowledge are effective ways to manage your manager.

There are a lot of different types of networking: in-person networking, social media networking, and referral networking. Tom Matthews, the residential realtor in Concord, Massachusetts who I mentioned in chapter seven, identified BNI, Business Networking International as an example of a referral networking organization. This chapter will primarily focus on in-person networking. However, this is not to overlook the power of social media, and the chapter will include some useful networking tactics for social media as well. According to *CNN*, "as of March 2017, Facebook has 1.94 billion MAU (monthly active users), which is about 25.86% of the world's population, and 1.28 DAU (daily active users) and LinkedIn has over 500 million members globally."[9] Those numbers are astonishing.

Social media networking encroaches on both your personal networking and professional networking areas. Social media, professionally speaking, serves as your multimedia resume. It is your resume, your soapbox, and your references. And these private and professional worlds overlap, so be mindful about how you present yourself in these venues. But, to get back to networking, in all its sources, we will answer the question on what the value, purpose, and the "why" to the importance of networking.

Here is a breakdown of why networking is critical and what you can gain and potentially lose by not networking. The benefits consist of increased opportunities, increased shared knowledge, increased connections and increased visibility—being at the table. And the losses are just the opposite; if you don't network you will miss opportunities, miss shared knowledge, miss vital connections, and lose your spot at the table; becoming invisible. So the benefits of networking clearly outweigh any drawbacks. However, doing it can create a lot of angst and anxiety for some.

Now here are some networking realities: if people do not know who you are and what you do, they are not going to call you, connect, and reach out to you. In a study conducted by Lou Adler[10], CEO of Performance-Based Hiring Learning in 2016, he found that even for passive and less active job seekers, networking was their primary means of obtaining new employment. The study found that 85% of all jobs are filled via networking and the most interesting and surprising outcome of the study was that of all four groups researched; under/unemployed

9   *Facebook and Linkedin Stats of 2017. http://www.soravjain.com/facebook-linkedin-stats-facts-2017*

10   *Adler, Lou. "New Survey Reveals 85% of All Jobs are Filled Via Networking." LinkedIn. https://www.linkedin.com/pulse/new-survey-reveals-85-all-jobs-filled-via-networking-lou-adler/ 29 Feb 2016.*

active seekers, employed and active seekers, employed but those quiet "tiptoe" seekers, and employed passive seekers, in each group identified networking trumped all other forms of job sourcing. Networking has real and measurable value.

The other benefits about networking are that when you put yourself out there and let people know who you are and how you can be of service to them, you will be surprised at the doors and opportunities that open. Just like any other skill development, practice makes perfect. The more you do it the better you become at it and the higher level of confidence you will build. Now I do not want to say that you will find a love for networking. Rather, you will find it more tolerable; with quality outcomes over time and you may find that it can even a tad bit fun. Okay, maybe now I am pushing it, but nonetheless, networking may be the catalyst for new, favorable circumstances.

First, let's explore and identify who are your current networking communities. Below is a diagram of a networking community chart. In this diagram, you are in the center. All of the boxes outside are your networking connections. Take a few minutes to identify your communities; it may be family, friends, maybe a club, or an association that you belong to. Identify all of the communities and entities that you are connected with. When you have finished, take a look at all of the people that are embodied within each of your networking communities. I bet you have at least 50 people captured in the entire diagram and possibly up to several hundred.

Who are my networking communities?

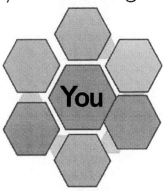

Now, think about getting together with one other person; your spouse or partner, your close friend or a colleague and visualize both of your networking community diagrams sitting side by side. How many people would you now have in your networking community? A hundred? Maybe several hundred? Possibly more than a thousand? And add another person, now you multiply that number and your networking reach grows exponentially. Get the idea? Networking expands your tentacles and the connections that could assist you on your journey. It is helpful to have a visual aid to see who is involved in your networking community and the networking communities of other people that you know. It allows you to capture on paper all of the groups that could represent possible connections.

We cannot dispute the impact that networking has and the potential opportunities that may exist as a result, however, some of us hate, detest, or just loathe the concept and thought of networking. I mean it just may push us out of our comfort zone and straight into a panic zone. Just curious—why is that? Well, it may have to do with the fact that as many as 50% of us are introverts. And, as being an introvert does not mean that we are anti-social. It does not mean we are anti-constant conversation. It does not mean that introverts are necessarily shy. Shyness is the fear of social disapproval or humiliation, while introversion is a preference for environments that are not overstimulating. Shyness can be inherently painful; introversion is not. So, in essence, introverts can get drained just being around a high stimulation environment, like a networking event, and that may be the barrier you have to overcome.

Being an introvert versus being an extrovert is really just talking about how we recharge our batteries. Introverts need to re-juice and re-charge in a smaller, more private way, rather than being amongst a loud, large social event. We can be social but it will drain us more quickly than compared with our extrovert friends. If you are an introvert or the qualities shared sound like you, according to research, introverts can actually be more effective leaders. Being an introvert does not need to be your deterrent for not attending networking events. It can truly be your ally. As introverts, you are often a better listener; with this in mind, attack the networking challenge by being yourself. The only person you can really bring to the table is your authentic self and why not—you are fabulous just the way you are! A façade will eventually be unveiled!

So let's review and create a networking strategy, a plan of attack to develop this skill set and bust through your worries about networking. Remember, networking is a skill. It can be developed and mastered over time just like any other aptitude or technique. And in every technique you wish to build competence in, you first have to adjust your mindset, identify the what, when, and where, get prepared, adopt an approach, and utilize a follow-up method system. Voila, those are the steps we are going to use in our networking strategy.

Let's first start with your mindset. Networking does not need to be viewed or seen as a transactional or "sales-y" process. I have often heard others describe networking as superficial conversational, a time when they have to sell themselves and create an image that doesn't fit who they are. I challenge you to translate networking in your mind as a way of helping people, your way of giving to others, your way of serving for the betterment of others. As we know, in relationships there is a rotation of giving and receiving. If all you do and focus on is "to take" from your relationships they will eventually lose their potency. But those individuals, the people who give, and give without the pretense of getting, will reap the benefits organically. The dynamic shifts when you see networking as an opportunity to explore what you can do to help others. Begin with a giving mindset and an attitude of walking in with the intention of finding ways of furnishing others with your gifts and talents.

Next, you want to research and locate what, when, and where networking opportunities are occurring. You can start with your current networking communities and see if there are networking events that they are offering or hosting. Ask your friends, family, or colleagues if they know of any upcoming events. Check on-line to see if there are any events published on sites such as MeetUp.com or Google networking events in your industry. You will be surprised at the number of events and workshops that you will stumble upon. You may also utilize social gatherings as networking opportunities such as family and friend gatherings. Target a goal around networking. Identify a certain number of events that you would like to attend over the next year. Is it one every other month? Once a month? You decide and again, remind yourself, this is not a sales mission, and it is a giving opportunity.

Once you identify your target number and the networking events that you will attend, as they approach, get prepared; have business cards ready and identify your goals. What may be some good goals you can set for a networking event? Well, it may be as simple as handing out ten business cards, getting ten business cards, speaking to a particular person that you know may show up, practicing your elevator pitch to five different people, and/or meeting three new people. Whatever your desired goal is, the purpose is to set your intention. Your goals may be varied based on the different events.

The next step is to come armed with an approach while at the networking event. The approach that I learned at BNI (the referral networking organization mentioned earlier) is: know, like, trust, buy. What does that mean exactly? Well, let's start with the first two (know and like) and the other two will flow (trust and buy). The premise is to focus on getting to know people. Keep your focus and energy on listening and getting to know the people you are meeting. Focus on building a rapport using your listening skills and being your genuine self. Now as much as I would like to think that I am a likable person, I know that most people that I encounter, in fact, like me, but I am confident that I have come across a lot of people in my lifetime that are not thrilled and that is A-OKAY. You may encounter the same thing, and you just have to understand that you may not be able to win them all of the time.

As you enter a networking event, what do we usually do? Look for folks we know, look at our phones. We continue to look at our phones, and then after about 15 minutes when we are not talking to anyone, we leave and we say what a waste of time! Instead, scan the room and watch the body language of the group. You will usually see folks in a group, and you can scan their body language to gauge what message their body language is communicating. Either they will be in an "open" posture or a "closed" posture. The open posture is one that you feel invited to walk into and the other one, closed, feels like you are shut out and unable to penetrate that group. When you assess the message, whom should you approach? The single person? Well, maybe they will be interesting and could offer a great connection, but they are one person. The two are double the number, but a group of three offers a greater net. If there are three who are demonstrating an open posture and there is a woman—yes women are natural includers—approach that group. And ask, "May I join you?" And then "shut up"! Slowly close the group physically and now you have strategically formed a networking circle.

So, now we will move onto the like part of our approach. Use this acronym WAIT: Why Am I Talking? If you are not listening, you are not learning and if you are not learning, you are not listening. Be interested before being interesting. Or as Steven Covey would say, "Seek to understand before you are to be understood." It's relational. How you make people feel will have an impact on the impressions and perception that is received about you. So, listen on. Keep your focus. Remember why you are there and your goal. Start off with know and like; trust and buy will flow naturally.

We often see people make the mistake of meeting many individuals at networking events and then not having a system in place to follow up with the new contacts afterward. Here's a simple follow-up formula I recommend; it's called the 24/7/30 System.

When you meet someone at a networking event, drop him or her a note within the first 24 hours. It can be a personal handwritten note or an email. Use whatever approach you will do consistently. Let them know that it was a pleasure meeting him or her and you hope your paths cross again.

Within 7 days, connect with them on social media. Make a connection via LinkedIn or Facebook. Follow them on Twitter or join them on Google+. Find ways to connect and engage with them via the social media platforms you use the most. Do not do this as a way to sell to them; do it as a way to start establishing a meaningful connection with them.

Within 30 days, reach out to them to set up a face-to-face meeting. If you live near each other, meet in person. If you are far away from one another, set up a meeting via Skype or by phone. At this meeting, find out more about what they do, and look for ways to help them in some way. Don't make it a sales call; make it a relationship-building opportunity.

Although networking may be at the bottom of your bucket list, it does have a proven track record. Seventy-two percent of people say their impressions[11] are impacted by how someone appears and their handshake[12] and of course that can only be done face to face and in person. In person networking savvy and proficiency can be created over time. Who knows, you might find that you get far more out of it than ever expected.

11 *"The Importance of Face to Face Networking." https://www.virgin.com/entrepreneur/info-graphic-the-importance-of-face-to-face-networking*

12 *"Face to Face Networking Stats." HubSpot. https://blog.hubspot.com/sales/face-to-face-net-working-stats*

Chapter 9

Compassion, kindness and a positive energetic attitude always prevail.

Practicing self-care by taking good care of your mental health and emotional attitude is key. The energy and attitude that you emanate has a huge impact on your day, affects how you feel internally and certainly affects those that we encounter. It will have a huge influence on our interactions, and especially with our managers. People like to be around those who are upbeat, positive, and enthusiastic. It's a downer to be around someone who is frumpy and negative. It can feel as though it is sucking all of your good energy right out of your sphere and leaving you feeling heavier. Being emotionally grounded and exuding a healthy and positive level of energy can go a long way. If nothing else, it will keep you in a positive circle mentally, physically, and spiritually.

So, where does a good attitude come from and how can I get one? Are you naturally born with a positive attitude? Is it something that you can develop and acquire if it does not appear naturally? And most importantly, how do I maintain a positive attitude even when things are not going so well. It's easy when things are going our way; when we feel at ease and at peace. The trickier times are when things feel rough and intense. How do we maintain a level of positivity when things are challenging?

Well, I don't know if I can answer all of those questions, but generally speaking from a self-identified and known "positive person" amongst my family, friends, and colleagues, I do believe it is an inside job and it begins every morning with a fresh start and a routinized morning structure. Yes, I said it. I do believe it begins with getting up in the morning and how you kick off your mornings. We can actually take this one step further and say it really begins with the night before. It is our nighttime routines that set the stage for preparing us for the morning ahead. And our morning routine sets the stage for how the day will unfold.

Let me tell you a story about setting the stage the night before. In the fall of 2011, I was training to run my third Boston Marathon through a charity organization. You see, in order to run the Boston Marathon and be eligible to run with an official number you have to qualify, meaning that you have had to have run qualifying races within a certain time frame for your age and gender. Honestly speaking, I qualified as an 80-year-old woman, which means that I run very, very slow. I am not ashamed of my running time; it is just a fact that I will always, inevitably be at the back of the pack. Unless of course, I am running with other 80-year-old women.

So, in order to train for the Boston Marathon, I participated in a 16-week training program from November through April's race day. As part of my training program I had to run five days a week anywhere between 18 miles and at the final stages of my training up to 38 miles per week. So, I was outside hitting the pavement a lot. And, since I live in New England, the weather from November through April is cold, snowy, and sometimes slushy. I would be running outside in tempera- tures in the teens and most often in the 20s. Yes, I know what you are thinking...that is frigid weather and wouldn't you rather be snuggled under your blankets in bed? Well, I ran in the morning because I am a morning person, so it was not only cold, but it was dark. And, to be perfectly blunt, I really was not *gung-ho* about getting up at 5 am five days week and heading out for a run ranging anywhere from 3–20 miles in the frigid New England winter air. But, I did it. And, the question is how. How did I get up for sixteen weeks, five days a week, and run all those miles 99% of the time? Well, the answer was simple. I had a compelling reason to do it and I prioritized my goal of getting to the start line on race day mentally, physically, and spiritually prepared. And it all began with what I did each night before.

Here is what I did. I would make sure that I got my workout clothes all ready and laid out the night before. I would get my coffee set up with my mug laid out on the counter. I would go to bed early enough so I got the right amount of sleep. I would read an inspirational quote before bed and lastly, I would post on my Facebook page to whom I was dedicating my morning run. Those were the tactics I used to get myself most prepared for my journey on the pavement the next morning.

The next step was when I woke up I would jump out of bed, brush my teeth, get my coffee ready, jump into my running gear, drink my cup of coffee, and then head out. I would operate almost like a machine. I did not think about it—I just did it. And, if you were to ask me, there was nothing at that time that indicated that I was positive, motivated, or even a tad bit excited about what I was about to encounter. I just did it. The interesting part was that as I would be on my run, maybe a mile or two or sometimes three into it, I would look around and realize how awesome it felt to be out there. How alive I felt to experience the sting of the wind and briskness of the cold slap my face into wakefulness and it would be then, at that point, that I was glad I was there and my motivation would kick in. I would then remember whom I was running for that day. I would envision that person and say a prayer for them and let them know inside my head that everything I was doing at that moment was in honor of them. The experience of training for the three Boston Marathons allowed me to develop a theory on motivation. Here it is… motivation is nonsense. Do it, and then the motivation will come. If you wait for that inspiring or explosive awakening to drive you into action, I am afraid to say that you may be waiting a long time. Again, do it and then you will get motivated. Action and movement create motivation.

So, what is your marathon that you are training for both literally and figuratively? What are the goals and targets you are striving for both personally and professionally? And what are some techniques and tips you can incorporate to enter each and every day in the best mental space possible so that ultimately you can maximize your effectiveness to achieve your goals and intentions? And how can you better and more masterfully manage your day, including managing your manager? It all begins with preparing the night before and creating a morning routine that will set you up for a successful day.

Here are some nighttime routine tips. Incorporate and test out even one or two of these to see if there is any benefit:

- Identify a regular bedtime schedule and try to adhere to it.

- Go to bed when you are tired and try to stick to a consistent time.

- Try setting the stage and transition into sleep at least one to hours before bedtime by dimming lights, setting out your clothes for the next day, and taking a hot bath or shower.

- Pack your lunch for the next day.

- Avoid stimulants or chemicals that will keep you awake: caffeine, nicotine, or alcohol. Instead, try drinking a non-caffeinated hot cup of tea or hot water with lemon.

- Keep the stimulation low. Turn down the lights, the volume of the noise on the radio, TV, and even the volume of our voices.

- Avoid watching TV. Instead, write in your journal about your day, read an article, book, or meditate.

- Write your daily to-do list for the following day.

- Ensure that you create the right environment for sleep in your bedroom. Consider the lighting, having a good mattress, and pillows.

Once you awaken, here are some morning routine tips. Again incorporate and test them out. Even if you add one or two to your routine you will reap benefits:

- Get up at your right time. Everyone is different. You may be a 5 a.m.'er or maybe you are a 6:30 a.m.'er. Regardless, wake up to your best-scheduled time.

- Don't stay in bed, awaken to the day and get out of bed as soon as you can.

- Avoid at all costs, looking at your phone. Have a "no phone" rule until at least an hour after you get up.

- Drink a cup of hot water with lemon. Move and hydrate.

- Exercise if you are a morning workout person or do some light stretches.

- Meditate or take a few minutes in quiet reflection to set your intentions for the day. Identify what and who are you are grateful for.

- Walk your dog.

- Shower or bathe.

- "Eat the frog."

Mark Twain once said, "If the first thing, you do each morning is to eat a live frog, you can go through the day with the satisfaction of knowing that that is probably the worst thing that is going to happen to you all day long."

What does that actually mean? Well, get what you are dreading most out of the way first thing, so the rest of the day feels like cherries on a cake. It is a good strategy and actually one that I employ, although I never really ate an actual frog. I purposely take on the items on my list for the day that I am trying to escape, which are perceived to be hard and difficult or are on my least favorite list. It does work. I tackle it first and then it's done.

Anchoring a consistent nighttime and morning routine will facilitate and help you launch into the next day focused, intentional, and in the right frame to take on your day. The more centered and focused your routines become the greater chance that your level of energy will rise to meet any occasion with vigor and balance. And that positive energy will put you in the mindset to make better and more productive decisions, especially in the way you relate to others, especially in the way in which you engage and present yourself to your loved ones, your friends, people in the workplace, and to your manager.

Resources

Adler, Lou. "New Survey Reveals 85% of All Jobs are Filled Via Networking." LinkedIn. https://www.linkedin.com/pulse/new-survey-reveals-85-all-jobs-filled-via-networking-lou-adler/ 29 February 2016.

Bolles, Richard N. What Color is My Parachute: 2017: A Practical Manual for Job-Hunters and Career-Changers. Brilliance Audio, 2017.

Business Networking International-Massachusetts. bnimass.com

Frost, Aja. "15 Surprising Stats on Networking and Face-to-Face Communication." HubSpot. https://blog.hubspot.com/sales/face-to-face-networking-stats.

Gajendran, Ravi and Somaya, Deepak. "Employees Leave Good Bosses Nearly as Often as Bad Ones." Harvard Business Review. https://hbr.org/2016/03/employees-leave-good-bosses-nearly-as-often-as-bad-ones

Soravjain. "Facebook and Linkedin Stats of 2017." http://www.soravjain.com/facebook-linkedin-stats-facts-2017. 17 August 2017.

Strengths Finder, Gallup. gallupstrengthcenter.com

Robins, Tony. "Why Meaning is Everything." https://www.tonyrobbins.com/why-meaning-is-everything/

Reh, F. John. https://www.linkedin.com/in/fjohnreh/ t

Reh, F. John. "Pareto's Principle: The 80-20 Rule." The Balance. *https://www.thebalance.com/pareto-s-principle-the-80-20-rule-2275148*. 08 August 2017.

Virgin. "The Importance of Face to Face Networking." https://www.virgin.com/entrepreneur/infographic-the-importance-of-face-to-face-networking

16419464R00036

Printed in Great Britain
by Amazon